JAMES K.
POLK

PRESIDENTIAL ◆ LEADERS

JAMES K. POLK

CAROL H. BEHRMAN

LERNER PUBLICATIONS COMPANY/MINNEAPOLIS

To Edward, my favorite historian, who is really the coauthor of
this book

Lerner Publications Company
A division of Lerner Publishing Group
241 First Avenue North
Minneapolis, MN 55401 U.S.A.

Website address: www.lernerbooks.com

Library of Congress Cataloging-in-Publication Data

Behrman, Carol H.
    James K. Polk / by Carol H. Behrman.
        p.   cm. — (Presidential leaders)
    Includes bibliographical references and index.
    ISBN: 0–8225–1396–X (lib. bdg. : alk. paper)
    1. Polk, James K. (James Knox), 1795–1849—Juvenile literature. 2. Presidents—United
States—Biography—Juvenile literature. I. Title. II. Series.
E417.B44 2005
973.6'1'092—dc22   2004017729

Manufactured in the United States of America
1 2 3 4 5 6 – JR – 10 09 08 07 06 05

J 973.61

P769 ⟨B⟩

CONTENTS

The office of Dr. Ephraim McDowell, who performed an operation on sixteen-year-old Polk, still stands in Danville, Kentucky.

INTRODUCTION

A NEW LEASE ON LIFE

*I closed my education at a later
period of life than is usual... having
been much afflicted... [with] very
bad health in my youth.*

—James Polk

The doctor opened his surgical kit and removed several sharp, gleaming instruments. He glanced at the patient stretched out on a table across the room. His assistants had used heavy ropes to lash the boy securely to the wooden tabletop.

Dr. Ephraim McDowell took his time getting ready. He was in no rush to begin. The procedure he was about to perform was dangerous. The chance for success was not good, even though he was a renowned and skillful surgeon. In 1812 most patients who were operated upon died from infections or blood poisoning. Doctors then didn't know how to prevent such deaths.

In this case, surgery was the only option. Sixteen-year-old Jim had been frail and sickly during his entire childhood. For years weakness and severe stomach pains had made it impossible for him to lead a normal life. Jim came from an educated family, but his illness had kept him from attending school. He could barely read and write.

His symptoms had finally become so severe that he and his father had made a grueling, 230-mile trip from Tennessee to Kentucky to consult with the famous surgeon. Dr. McDowell diagnosed Jim's problem as a buildup of minerals in the urinary tract (urinary stones). The stones had to be removed through surgery. Jim's only hope for recovery lay in the surgeon's capable hands.

Dr. McDowell instructed his assistants to give Jim a drink of brandy. It would dull the terrible pain of surgery somewhat. Besides alcohol, doctors had no other painkillers in 1812. The doctor picked up a scalpel (surgical knife) and prepared to cut. His aides held the patient down tightly to prevent him from moving.

To everyone's relief, the frail teenager survived the operation. Jim recovered and knew the joy of being healthy and free of pain for the first time in his memory. He even enjoyed showing his friends and family the stones the doctor had removed. They had been the cause of many of his childhood woes.

Afterward, James Knox Polk could hope for a full and productive life. But no one then dreamed that his achievements would include becoming president of the United States.

CHAPTER ONE

THE FARM BOY

It was here that I received lessons . . .
to which I attribute whatever
success . . . has attended me.

—James Polk, discussing his university education

James Knox Polk, known to his family as Jim, was born in Mecklenburg County, in western North Carolina, on November 2, 1795. His parents were Samuel and Jane Knox Polk. Their Scotch-Irish ancestors had immigrated to North America in the late 1600s. Jane was a descendant of John Knox, who had founded the Presbyterian Church in Scotland.

James was their first child. Samuel and Jane were Presbyterians, although Jane was stricter in her faith than her husband. She wanted her new son to be baptized—or initiated into the Presbyterian Church. She and Sam took the baby to the local pastor. But Sam was a strong-minded man. When he and the pastor got into an argument over

*Growing up, James learned about the local militiamen who
fought in the American Revolution.*

———————— ✧ ————————

commander, Lord Charles Cornwallis, to call the county a
"hornet's nest" of rebels. Heroes still walked among them
during Jim's boyhood. His grandfather Ezekial Polk had
served in the colonial militia—the army of colonists who
fought the British. He held the boy spellbound with stories
about brave revolutionaries in the struggle to establish the
United States of America.

Jim was a handsome boy with clear-cut features, dark
hair, and gray eyes. He was slender and small for his age,
and often sickly. But he enjoyed wandering along the
gently rolling hills that sloped down to Little Sugar
Creek. A neighbor recalled that "Little Jimmy Polk used

to pass along this road often...barefooted with his britches [pants] rolled up to his knees. He was a mighty bashful little fellow."

A NEW LIFE IN TENNESSEE

In 1806, when Jim was eleven, his parents decided to sell their farm and move west to Tennessee. Jim's grandfather Ezekial had resettled there several years earlier. He convinced Sam and Jane that good opportunities existed in the "Far West," as Tennessee was then called.

The journey to Tennessee was difficult and dangerous. By then Jim had four younger siblings—two sisters and two brothers, including an infant boy. The new home in Tennessee was five hundred miles away. They had to walk the whole distance, along with their heavily loaded wagons. It took a month and a half to trek through fields and valleys

────────────── ✧ ──────────────

Many families traveled west by wagon in the 1700s and 1800s.

and over the rugged Cumberland Mountains to the Duck River Valley near Nashville, Tennessee. There, the family settled on a large farm, where they planted corn and tobacco.

The Polk family was close and loving. In Tennessee, Sam and Jane had five more children, for a total of ten. Their farm was successful, and they grew prosperous. Sam and Jane brought up their children as strict Presbyterians. As part of this religious training, the children were taught to work hard and never waste time or complain.

Sam and Jane also taught their children about politics. They thought U.S. citizens had a responsibility to be informed and active in their communities. They believed in the democratic principles set forth in the Declaration of Independence and the U.S. Constitution—the principles of

◇ ——————————

The Declaration of
Independence

individual freedom and self-government—and they passed down these beliefs to their children.

A RISKY OPERATION

All was not well with the Polks' eldest son. Jim had always been sickly, and his health became worse each year. He suffered from severe stomach pains, nausea, and weakness. He tried diligently to do his chores on the farm but often did not have the strength to complete them. He was seldom well enough to attend school, so he could barely read and write. He could not take part in the rough play of other boys. They often made fun of him and called him a weakling. Jim became serious and reserved.

Local doctors were unable to diagnose Jim's ailment. Sam Polk was desperate to discover what was wrong with his son. So he took the sixteen-year-old boy to see a famous surgeon, Dr. Ephraim McDowell, in Danville, Kentucky. The long, rough trip on horseback was difficult for the sick boy but well worth the struggle. Dr. McDowell identified the problem as urinary stones and operated to remove them. The surgery was dangerous and painful, but Jim faced it with a toughness of mind and spirit. He began to feel better almost immediately. Jim recovered from the surgery and gradually became stronger and healthier than he had ever been.

OFF TO SCHOOL

Once Jim had recovered, his family began to plan his career. His father thought Jim should learn business skills. He sent him to a merchant about six miles from their home to work as an apprentice—a merchant in training. Jim hated the work. He had other ideas about his future.

More than anything else, Jim Polk wanted to become educated. He had suffered with pain and poor health for much of his life. He was determined to make up for his physical drawbacks by excelling in the use of his mind. Jim convinced his father to enroll him in a nearby Presbyterian school, the Zion Church Academy. It was run by Robert Henderson, a respected scholar. Here Jim Polk began his formal education. He was several years older than the other students and far behind in his lessons, but he studied diligently. By the end of his first year, he had mastered Greek, Latin, and English grammar. Jim not only caught up with the other boys, he surpassed them.

Jim was ready for greater challenges, so his parents sent him to a larger school, the Bradley Academy, in Murfreesboro, Tennessee. There he studied Greek, Latin, mathematics, literature, philosophy, astronomy, and geography. He was a top student at the academy and described by his teachers as "much the most promising young man in the school."

He made new friends there. One of his pals was Anderson Childress. Sometimes Anderson's mother invited Jim to their elegant home in Murfreesboro for dinner. Jim enjoyed the warmth and friendliness of the Childress family. They found him likable too. Anderson's eleven-year old sister, Sarah, amused the boys with her clever wit.

Several years later, James Polk successfully applied for admission to the University of North Carolina, one of the best colleges in the region. He scored so high on his entrance examinations that the university allowed him to skip his freshman (first) year.

Polk attended the Univesity of North Carolina at Chapel Hill.
This photograph of the campus was taken in 1902.

COLLEGE YEARS

In 1816 twenty-one-year-old Jim Polk entered the University of North Carolina at Chapel Hill. He was no longer an awkward, sickly loner but had grown into a healthy and confident young man. He was not tall—just five feet eight inches—but he was self-assured, polite, and well liked. He performed brilliantly in Latin, Greek, English literature, and other courses. He also wrote a prize-winning essay on American liberty.

While listening to his parents' political discussions back home, Jim had come to revere both Thomas Jefferson, the nation's third president and author of the Declaration of Independence, and Andrew Jackson, a former congressman, senator, and war hero. Their lives and work, especially their belief in the freedom and rights of citizens, strongly influenced his thoughts and decisions.

At school Jim continued his interest in politics. He joined a debating club, the Dialectic Society. The club members met weekly to discuss current affairs. Jim discovered that he had a gift for debate (discussing an issue by considering opposing—pro and con—arguments) and was elected president of the society. He began to think seriously about a career in law or politics, areas where he could best use his skills as a debater.

In June 1818, James Polk graduated from the University of North Carolina with high honors in mathematics and the classics (Greek and Latin). He was chosen to deliver the welcoming address in Latin at the school's graduation ceremonies. James had worked so hard in school that he had worn himself out. He again suffered from weakness and stomach problems. After graduation, he had to remain in Chapel Hill, where he rested for four months. Finally, he was well enough to go home to Tennessee, eager to get on with the next part of his life. James Polk had new and lofty dreams about the future.

CHAPTER TWO

THE YOUNG LAWYER

*[Polk's] thorough academic
preparation, his accurate knowledge of the
law, his readiness . . . in debate . . . secured
him . . . employment, and in less than a year he
was already a leading practitioner.*
—J. L. Martin, *Democratic Review,* 1838

By the time James Polk returned home in 1818, his father
had become wealthy through land speculation (buying and
selling). While his son was still at college, Sam had built a
large, two-story brick house for his family in Columbia,
Tennessee. Southwest of Nashville, Columbia was a busy
town with tree-lined streets, successful businesses, and fine
homes. James Polk moved into the house with his family.

By then he had settled on a career as a lawyer. At that
time, aspiring lawyers did not attend law school but instead
worked for experienced lawyers who gave them on-the-job
legal training. Polk was fortunate to find a position in the

*Polk became a lawyer
and was first introduced to
politics by working with lawyer
Felix Grundy (left).*
✧ ————————————

Nashville office of Felix Grundy. Grundy was a former Kentucky state congressman and one of Tennessee's leading lawyers, with a strong record of winning cases. Grundy took a liking to his serious, hardworking young student, and they became good friends. For a year, Polk worked in Nashville, studying with Grundy and poring over thick law books until late in the night.

In Tennessee then, most areas had too few people to have local lawyers. Lawyers such as Grundy traveled from town to town on horseback, pleading cases in courthouses around the state. Grundy sometimes took his apprentice with him.

In 1819, while Polk was traveling with Grundy, the United States faced severe economic problems. Crop prices fell due to competition from European farmers. Thousands of settlers who had purchased land on credit (borrowed money) couldn't repay their bank loans, so banks took over their farms, often leaving the settlers penniless. Farmers in Tennessee suffered great losses. Thomas Jefferson had said that government was best for ordinary people when it was small and not controlled by banks and land speculators. The suffering that Polk saw riding from town to town confirmed his belief in Jefferson's ideas.

In 1820 James Polk passed the Tennessee bar exam. This allowed him to practice in the state as a full-fledged lawyer. In Polk's first case, he defended his own father. Sam had lost his temper during an argument and was accused of hitting another man. Polk persuaded the judge to settle the case with Sam paying only a one-dollar fine. Soon after, Polk opened a law office in Columbia. He became known for his honesty and ability. His politeness and pleasant sense of humor made him popular with lawyers and judges as well as with clients.

With the help of his friend Grundy, Polk got a job as the clerk for the Tennessee State Senate. In this position, he took care of the mountains of paperwork that related to senate business. The job lasted only a few weeks each year, when the senate was in session. Polk had plenty of time for his own law practice, but his job as clerk allowed him to observe political action up close. Here he decided that his future lay in politics.

Grundy introduced his young friend to some of the most important people in the state. He even met the pride of Tennessee, General Andrew Jackson. Jackson had defeated the British at the Battle of New Orleans in the War of 1812 (1812–1815), and Democratic Party members were then urging him to seek the U.S. presidency. Jackson took an interest in the young lawyer James Polk, and they became good friends.

POLK IN LOVE

The Tennessee State Senate met in the state capital, Murfreesboro, where Polk had attended school at the Bradley Academy. There, Polk became reacquainted with the Childress family. Their daughter, Sarah, was by then a grown woman. James Polk had enjoyed her company and found her amusing when she was eleven years old. This time he fell in love.

Sarah Childress

Sarah Childress had grown into an elegant, bright-eyed beauty. She wore her black hair gathered behind her head, with long ringlets framing her face. Her social skills and intelligence were as striking as her appearance. She was popular, lively, and clever. Her wealthy parents had given her a far better education than was available to most young women then. As a teenager, she had attended the Moravian Female Academy in Salem, North Carolina, one of the best boarding schools in the country for young women. She had studied geography, history, music, drawing, and literature.

James was attracted to Sarah not only for her beauty but also for her intelligence. She shared his interest in government, and she supported his political career. Polk began to think about marrying and starting a family. He went for advice to a man whose wisdom and judgment he respected—Andrew Jackson. Polk did not mention Sarah's name as his potential wife, but Jackson was a close friend of the Childress family, and he knew of Polk's interest in the young woman. Jackson advised Polk to marry soon. Choose the woman "who will never give you any trouble! . . . You know her well," Jackson said. He was of course referring to Sarah Childress. Sarah soon agreed to marry James.

In 1822 Polk decided to become a candidate for the Tennessee House of Representatives—one of that state's two lawmaking bodies (the other was the Tennessee State Senate). Polk campaigned all over his district. He traveled on horseback through villages and across miles of rough countryside to scattered settlements. He rode for hours at a time, sometimes through mud and pouring rain. In the United States at the time, only white men were allowed to vote. So Polk addressed his words to this audience. He

In the 1800s, politicians campaigned by traveling around the countryside and giving spirited speeches to small groups of people.

talked about issues that concerned farmers and businessmen, such as crop prices, taxes, and education. This kind of campaigning was called stumping because candidates often spoke to small gatherings while standing on top of tree stumps.

James Polk was an excellent speaker. His style was forceful, and his arguments were convincing. Short and slender, Polk had pleasing features with deep-set, penetrating gray eyes, a high forehead, high cheekbones, and a somewhat large nose. He wore his unruly black hair long and combed straight back. Before long, admirers were calling him the Napoleon of the Stump, after the French general Napoleon Bonaparte, who was also short but eloquent. Polk won the election by a wide margin. In August 1823, he took his seat in the state legislature.

On New Year's Day of 1824, he and Sarah Childress were married. Polk was twenty-eight years old. His bride was twenty. The Polk-Childress wedding was a great social event. Friends and relatives threw parties at their homes. The wedding was held at the Childress plantation—a large farm in Murfreesboro. Guests first enjoyed an elegant, seven-course dinner. Then the couple was married in a solemn religious service, conducted by a Presbyterian minister.

After several days of celebrations, the young couple began their married life in a two-room, rented house near Polk's parents' home in Columbia. Sarah did not mind living in a small home, she said. It required little housekeeping work and gave her more time to spend with her husband. She frequently helped Polk with his duties in nearby Murfreesboro.

TENNESSEE LAWMAKER

Soon after his election to the Tennessee House of Representatives, Polk had to make a major decision. Tennessee's politicians were split into two main factions (groups). Congressman John Overton, the richest, most important man in the state, led one of these groups. He looked out for the interests of big landowners, businesses, and banks. For many years, Overton had controlled politics in Tennessee. Recently, however, a new governor who opposed Overton had been elected. His name was William Carroll, and he became the leader of the other main faction in the legislature, one that worked for the interests of small farmers and laborers.

Polk's father, Sam, was a wealthy landowner and an Overton supporter. He also served on the board of directors of a bank owned by Overton. James Polk was expected to join his father and other Overton followers, but he didn't. The small farmers and laborers of the state had elected James Polk. He felt he had to stand behind them and decided to support Governor Carroll. In the Tennessee legislature, he spoke in favor of bills that would benefit ordinary people and provide better education for their children.

Polk was soon recognized as an effective speaker who usually came out on top in any debate. He found admirers and important allies as a legislator. Davy Crockett, an explorer and adventurer from the western frontier, served in the legislature with Polk. They usually worked together to

✧ ————————
Davy Crockett was a frontiersman, a Tennessee lawmaker, and a U.S. Congress member.

carry out Carroll's policies. Polk's teacher, Felix Grundy, was on the opposite side. Polk and Grundy often faced off in intense debates, but they remained good friends.

Polk was most proud of his friendship with his longtime hero, Andrew Jackson. They agreed on many important issues of the time and shared a deep concern for the welfare of common people. By then a twice-elected U.S. senator, General Jackson declared that he was a candidate for president in 1824.

Again, Polk faced a big decision. Overton and Grundy had decided to back Jackson, even though his ideas were the opposite of theirs. They hoped that backing Jackson, a popular candidate, would increase their own popularity in Tennessee and help them regain some of the power they had lost to Carroll and Polk. Governor Carroll supported a different candidate.

Polk wrestled with a difficult problem. His ally Davy Crockett was staying with the Carroll forces and opposing Jackson. But Polk could not bring himself to follow Crockett's example. He supported Andrew Jackson, against the wishes of his own faction. Polk was risking his political career, but he believed that the country needed Andrew Jackson as president. In the election, however, Jackson narrowly lost his bid for the presidency. The winner was John Quincy Adams.

CANDIDATE FOR CONGRESS

Andrew Jackson encouraged James Polk to run for the U.S. Congress, where he could work more effectively for Jackson's next presidential campaign. Sarah was enthusiastic about the plan, so Polk was soon stumping again, traveling

long hours while campaigning for national office. He was
much better educated than most of the farmers, traders,
and small shopkeepers of the area, but he respected them
and spoke simply and directly. He often made his point
through humor and amusing stories. Audiences responded
to his sincerity and concern for their problems. They
believed that he would look out for their interests. Polk's
efforts paid off, and he was elected to represent Tennessee's
sixth district in the U.S. House of Representatives.

CHAPTER THREE

CONGRESSMAN POLK

*This is a government based upon the will of
the People . . . all power emanates [comes] from
them . . . and . . . a majority should rule.*

—Congressman James Polk

James K. Polk left for Washington, D.C., in the fall of
1825. He was twenty-nine years old, one of the youngest
members of Congress. Sarah did not accompany him. The
couple had been warned that Washington did not have
decent housing and social activities for women. There
were no female members of Congress then. Women were
not allowed to vote, let alone run for office. Most law-
makers went to Washington alone, without their wives
and families.

Polk made the long journey along with other congressmen from Tennessee. They traveled on horseback through
the mountains and valleys of Tennessee, then along the
National Road, a major east-west road, to Baltimore,

Polk and the other Tennessee congressmen finished their journey to Washington, D.C., by stagecoach.

Maryland. There, they made arrangements to board their horses in stables. They would return for the horses in March, at the end of the congressional session. The forty-mile trip from Baltimore to Washington was made by stagecoach.

Washington was not yet a glistening, marble-filled city. It was unfinished and uncomfortable. Much of the city had been burned to the ground by British troops during the War of 1812 and had not yet been rebuilt. The white-domed Capitol building was still under construction. Most streets, including Pennsylvania Avenue, site of the White House, were filled with dry, choking dust in summer and were deep in mud during winter.

Polk and other congressmen from Tennessee rented rooms in a boardinghouse. Each man had a private room in which to sleep, work, and see visitors. The men ate together at a long table in the house's dining room. In the evening, they wrote letters or held lively conversations about politics and world problems.

In Washington, James Polk was at the center of the nation's political power. There, he would participate in making laws. He hoped to help the people of his district who had elected him. Most of all, he wanted to carry out the policies and ideals of Andrew Jackson.

Polk met the challenge of being a congressman the way he had always faced difficulties. He worked hard to do the best possible job. He studied daily, often far into the night, learning parliamentary procedure (the rules by which the House of Representatives was run). Polk examined every detail of proposals and bills. He attended every session of Congress, always ready to take a stand on any issue. Other congressmen noted the small, courteous Tennessean's attention to detail. They began to seek his advice when they needed information.

A FRESH VOICE IN CONGRESS

John Quincy Adams was president of the United States. He had beaten Andrew Jackson in a close and bitter election in 1824. Jackson had won the popular vote, but no candidate had received a majority of votes in the Electoral College—a system by which state electors (representatives) choose the president, based only in part on the popular vote. According to rules governing elections, the House of Representatives decided who would become president, and it chose Adams.

John Quincy Adams was president when Polk arrived in Congress.
——————— ✧

Jackson's followers believed that Adams's supporter, Henry Clay, had used bribery and secret promises to persuade members of the House to choose Adams. They suspected fraud and corruption. Even worse, Adams then appointed Clay as secretary of state. It appeared as though the two men had worked together to advance both their political careers.

The Jackson people were outraged. They immediately began a campaign to ensure General Jackson's election four years later. In Congress Jackson's supporters opposed Adams's administration in every possible way. James K. Polk soon became one of the leaders of this opposition.

Polk delivered his first major speech in Congress on March 13, 1826. He spoke in favor of a proposal to prevent this sort of disputed outcome in future presidential races. The proposal involved changing the U.S. Constitution, so that the candidate with the most popular votes became president—then races would no longer be decided by the Electoral College or the House of Representatives.

Polk's speech was brief and to the point, at a time when most politicians gave flowery and long-winded speeches. Polk spoke in a clear, low-pitched voice. He had carefully studied all the legal issues and presented his conclusions in a clear, reasonable manner. He said that the president represented all the people and should be chosen directly by them.

President Adams and his supporters opposed Polk's proposal. They didn't think that uninformed and sometimes poorly educated citizens should have the final say in choosing the president. Adams had many supporters in Congress, and the resolution was defeated. But James Polk had made an impression as a clear thinker who should be taken seriously.

A NEW ROLE FOR SARAH POLK

In the spring of 1826, at the end of the congressional session, Polk returned to his home in Tennessee. He and Sarah had been apart for six long months. When it was time to go to Washington again in the fall, Sarah insisted on going with him. They traveled comfortably in their own stagecoach, accompanied by another Tennessee congressman, Sam Houston.

In Washington the Polks stayed a few days at Williamson's Hotel. Then they rented a two-room suite in a boardinghouse for married couples. The suite had a large, drafty bedroom and a barely furnished parlor. Sarah brightened up the home with a piano and fresh curtains. They also kept a home in Tennessee, living there when Congress wasn't in session.

Sarah's presence in Washington made a big difference for her husband. James Polk was quiet. He cared most about his responsibilities as a member of Congress but did not care much for socializing. His wife was just the opposite. She was outgoing and friendly. She loved to give and attend parties. She was a popular hostess and guest. Her charming personality and elegance helped her husband make contacts that were valuable for his career.

Sarah also took a lively interest in politics. Sometimes, after dinner parties, Sarah did not retire to another room with the women, as was the custom. Instead, she chose to remain with the men, and she listened avidly while they smoked cigars and discussed the vital issues of the day. Almost daily, she sat in the gallery (visitors' area) of the House of Representatives and watched the congressmen discuss proposals. Her knowledge of politics and national issues increased. Before long, Sarah became her husband's chief adviser.

SECOND-TERM CONGRESSMAN

The voters in Polk's district elected him to Congress again in 1827. He was recognized as one of Andrew Jackson's main supporters, and his friendship with his mentor deepened. Jackson remained at home in Tennessee throughout John Quincy Adams's term in office. He began to rely more and more upon Polk for information about events in Washington. The two men exchanged many letters, and the general often expressed his confidence in his young ally.

James Polk was a rising star. During his second term in Congress, he was appointed to the influential Committee on Foreign Affairs. This job put him in a position to block Adams's administration on many issues concerning U.S. relations with other countries.

Polk suffered a grievous personal loss when his father died in November 1827. James inherited a large portion of Samuel Polk's estate (including money, the family home, household slaves, and other possessions) as well as major responsibilities. As the eldest of ten children, he became the new head of the family. He and Sarah had to look after the welfare of his aging mother and the extended family. Several of Polk's brothers were untrustworthy and irresponsible. They got into legal and financial trouble regularly. James and Sarah had to solve many problems and straighten out the affairs of his family.

Meanwhile, Andrew Jackson's second campaign for the presidency went into high gear. New political parties emerged. The group that supported Adams for a second term was first called the National Republicans, then the Whigs. Jackson's party became the Democrats. Polk campaigned vigorously for the general. He believed Jackson would represent the interests of the common citizen. He traveled ceaselessly across Tennessee on horseback, rallying voters. It was a dirty campaign. Andrew Jackson's enemies hurled nasty accusations against him, including attacks on his military career and on the character of his wife, Rachel. Polk helped Jackson by digging up evidence to prove that these charges were false. He continued to oppose the policies of John Quincy Adams in Congress.

Andrew Jackson (left) was inaugurated at the
U.S. Capitol on March 29, 1829.

THE JACKSON PRESIDENCY

In 1828 Andrew Jackson successfully beat John Quincy Adams in the presidential election. He received an overwhelming majority, with 140,000 more votes than Adams, as well as two-thirds of the Electoral College. Jackson was called the people's president. Noisy crowds flowed into Washington to celebrate the election of their hero, shouting for Old Hickory, as Jackson was also called. Folks from all walks of life attended the inaugural ball at the White House.

James Polk in Congress worked in harmony with Andrew Jackson in the White House to achieve their common goals.

Most of their policies favored workers and small farmers against the forces of big business and finance. Together, they defeated a proposal to use federal (national government) money to build a road in Kentucky. Polk and Jackson believed that each state should pay for its own improvements, such as roads.

One of Polk's most important fights during the 1828–1829 session concerned a Tennessee land bill. The federal government owned large parcels of land in Tennessee. The land bill called for the property to be given to the state for schools and other educational purposes. Polk had introduced this bill during his first term. At first, all the congressmen from Tennessee had supported it. But during this term, one of these representatives, Davy Crockett, suddenly opposed the bill.

Democrats believed that Andrew Jackson's enemies were behind Crockett's complaints. The debate over the land bill became entangled with the strong feelings about the presidential campaign. Jackson's supporters felt betrayed by their fellow Tennessean. Once friends, Polk and Crockett exchanged bitter words on the floor of Congress. Crockett savagely attacked both Jackson and Polk. He was able to block passage of the land bill with the help of the Adams faction in Congress. Jackson's many supporters in Tennessee never forgave Crockett for his disloyalty.

By then James Polk was an influential member of the government. He was appointed to the Ways and Means Committee, an important committee that controls the raising of federal funds and how they are used. Even opponents respected his knowledge and understanding of complex issues. They appreciated his clear, straightforward arguments.

POLK'S FRIEND AND TEACHER

James Polk and his friend Andrew Jackson had much in common. Both were of Scotch-Irish descent. They were born, many years apart, on the western frontier of North Carolina. Most of their lives and careers were spent in Tennessee. They came from hardworking farm families and never forgot their roots among the common people.

They were quite different in appearance and personality. Polk was of medium height, quiet, serious, and reserved. Jackson was tall and athletic, with flaming red hair and a temper to match. He was active, outgoing, and bold.

Andrew Jackson had a difficult childhood. His father died before he was born, and his mother died while he was still a teenager. At fifteen, he enlisted in the Continental Army and fought against the British in the American Revolution. Afterward, Jackson studied law. He moved to Nashville, where he married the daughter of a prominent family. He became a successful attorney, then a judge, then a U.S. congressman.

Jackson led the Tennessee militia and the U.S. Army in successful wars against Native American nations. His courage and leadership in battle inspired the troops who served under him. They gave him the nickname Old Hickory, after the strongest wood in the forest. Jackson fought the British again in the War of 1812, leading his troops to a stunning victory in the Battle of New Orleans.

Jackson was elected the seventh president of the United States and served for two terms, from 1829 to 1837. As president, he managed to reduce corruption in government, pay off the national debt, crush the power of the Bank of the United States, and force southern states to accept national laws. He was the driving force behind the Democratic Party and continued as its undisputed leader until his death.

Many people hated and despised Jackson. The wealthy and powerful sneered at his common background. They fought against the reforms he pushed through that restricted their influence. He also made enemies with his fiery temper. He lashed out at anyone who insulted him or his family. He even fought duels (fights with pistols) to defend his honor.

Andrew Jackson also had many devoted and loyal followers, including James K. Polk. Both men believed that preserving the Union (United States) was more important than the wishes of individual states. And both believed that the role of government was to protect the interests of common citizens.

✧ ──────────────
Andrew Jackson (left) and Polk were devoted friends.

But family responsibilities continued to plague him. In 1831 Polk's twenty-eight-year-old brother, Frank, died of alcoholism. Two other brothers, Marshall and John, fell ill and died soon after. It was a terrible time for the family. James and Sarah felt these losses even more keenly since they did not have children of their own. (Historians believe that Polk's surgery for urinary stones as a teenager may have damaged his reproductive organs and left him unable to father children.)

The couple handled their grief by plunging more deeply into politics. They continued to live in their boardinghouse suite. James also pursued some business investments, unrelated to his work in Congress. He bought several pieces of property around the nation, including plantations (worked by slaves) in Tennessee and Mississippi.

BACKING JACKSON

By the early 1830s, a fight was brewing in Congress. The Bank of the United States was the most powerful financial institution in the country. It issued notes (paper money), made loans, and held deposits from big organizations, including the U.S. government. It also had the power to keep state banks from making certain loans or issuing too much money. President Jackson believed that the bank had too much power over the nation's money supply. He also believed its managers were corrupt and that its policies favored big business. He encouraged the development of local banks that would lend money to farmers, workers, and small businesses. Congressman Polk agreed.

In 1832 the Bank of the United States applied to Congress to have its charter (operating papers) renewed.

Henry Clay, who was running against Jackson in his bid for a second term as president, backed the effort. But President Jackson vetoed—refused to sign—the bank's application. He withdrew a large amount of U.S. government money from the bank and placed it in local state banks, called pet banks. A major battle began. The followers of both Jackson and Clay exchanged bitter insults in Congress and in the press. Most of Congress opposed the president's actions. Some Democrats refused to support him and switched to the other party.

James Polk remained loyal. He made a speech on behalf of Jackson that attracted national attention. In his speech, he presented details and examples that proved the bank was a tool of big business. He also showed convincing evidence that the bank was inefficient and corrupt. With Polk's help, Andrew Jackson succeeded in shutting down the bank. He was elected to a second term as president by a large majority.

Another battle facing Congress in the early 1830s concerned tariffs, or taxes on foreign goods coming into the United States. In 1828 Congress had passed a law that increased tariffs. With increased tariffs, foreign merchants were forced to charge more for their products sold in the United States. Northerners, whose economy was based on manufacturing, liked the high tariffs. They kept low-priced foreign goods off the market. This meant more people bought U.S.-made products. But southerners, whose economy was based on farming not manufacturing, wanted low-cost foreign products.

Congress voted to raise tariffs again in 1832. This vote upset many southerners. Their leader, John C. Calhoun of

South Carolina, argued that states should be able to nullify (ignore) federal laws with which they disagreed. Calhoun even threatened that South Carolina would secede, or withdraw, from the Union if federal agents tried to enforce the tariff laws in his state.

Both Jackson and Polk were southerners. They opposed tariffs too. But they believed that the future of the country depended on an unbreakable Union. Jackson took strong measures to enforce the new tariff—threatening to send troops into states that refused to follow the law. Again, Polk threw his support behind the president. Calhoun and his followers in the South backed down. For the time being, Jackson and Polk's strong stand avoided a crisis.

CHAPTER FOUR

SPEAKER OF THE HOUSE

*I have never seen a man preside over a popular
legislative body with more dignity and
effect than Mr. Polk.*

—*Nashville Union*, July 17, 1839

James Polk had become a leader in the House of Representatives. In 1834 he decided to run for that body's highest position, Speaker of the House.

The Speaker of the House is the leader of the majority party (the party with the most members) in the House of Representatives. The Speaker decides which bills should be sent to committee, appoints committee members, and schedules bills for discussion and voting. During debates, the Speaker grants members the right to speak. These powers make the Speaker of the House one of the most powerful people in Congress.

In his run for Speaker of the House, Polk was opposed by Congressman John Bell, also a Democrat from

John Bell
✧ ——————————

Tennessee. Like Polk, he had endorsed Andrew Jackson for president. To gain votes for his election as Speaker, however, Bell accepted support from Jackson's enemies in the Whig Party. He promised to join them in opposing President Jackson's programs. These extra votes decided the election, and Bell became Speaker of the House. He also joined the Whig Party.

The race for Speaker was the beginning of a political feud. From then on, Bell and Polk bitterly opposed one another in Congress. Back in Tennessee, between congressional sessions, they continued to argue over local and national issues. Both Jackson and Polk were angered by Bell's desertion (abandonment) of the Democratic Party. They considered him a traitor.

Polk continued to fight Old Hickory's battles in Congress. He and the president became even closer, politically and personally. More than ever, Polk was considered the president's leading voice in the House. His supporters were able to paint Speaker Bell as disloyal and untrustworthy. A year later, in December 1835, a new election was held for Speaker. This time, James Polk won.

As the Speaker of the House, James Polk was at the top of Washington society. He and Sarah had to change their lifestyle. It was difficult to receive important guests in their small boardinghouse lodgings, so they moved to a larger suite of rooms on Pennsylvania Avenue.

Sarah was happy in the role of hostess. She became famous for her social gatherings, and invitations to the Polk home were highly sought after. Even political enemies such as Henry Clay enjoyed the Polks' hospitality. James Polk bought a fashionable private coach for their travels around Washington.

GAG RULES

Partisan (party-based) politics grew more intense in the late 1830s. One controversial issue was slavery—the practice of white masters owning, buying and selling, and controlling the lives and labor of black Americans. The northern states had all abolished (outlawed) slavery by the 1830s, and some northerners wanted to outlaw slavery everywhere in the United States. Abolitionists said that slavery was inhumane and immoral. They railed against the cruel treatment that many slaves received from their white masters. Yet slavery continued in the South, where most slaves worked as farm laborers.

After James Polk became Speaker of the House, John Bell and former president John Quincy Adams, who had become a congressman, presented many petitions (formal requests), trying to introduce a bill abolishing slavery

This political cartoon depicts how heated debates on the issue of slavery sometimes turned into physical fights in the House of Representatives.

nationwide. They believed their cause was just, as did many northerners, but they also knew that their petitions would stir up anger among southern congressmen. With each new petition, debates between proslavery and antislavery forces raged in the House of Representatives. The constant fighting took up time and blocked discussion of other important issues. Violent fights even broke out on the floor of the House. Members began to arm themselves with knives.

James Polk's own attitudes about slavery were contradictory. The Polk family owned many slaves. Some worked as household servants. Others worked on Polk's plantations in Tennessee and Mississippi. But although he owned slaves, James Polk stated publicly that he thought slavery was wrong. He also predicted that the practice would eventually die out, without government action. When speaking about slavery, Polk always chose his words carefully, trying not to offend either northerners or southerners. Rather than taking a firm stand one way or the other, he seemed to want to avoid the issue.

To keep the slavery debate from getting in the way of other House business, in 1836 Polk and his supporters passed the first in a series of rules stating that all petitions regarding slavery would be sent to a special committee. The committee, staffed by Polk's supporters, then kept the petitions from reaching the House floor. Thus the rulings became known as gag rules because they gagged, or silenced, debate on slavery.

————————————— ✧ —————————————

Many people in the South thought slavery was necessary for running large plantations, such as this cotton plantation on the Mississippi River.

Polk's opponents were outraged. They began to make savage personal attacks upon him. One of his critics even challenged him to a duel. Polk ignored the vicious words and calmly continued presiding over the business of the House of Representatives.

Although the gag rules quashed debate in the House about slavery, they could not end the strong feelings on both sides of the issue. The problem continued to smolder. Meanwhile, despite unending opposition, Speaker Polk successfully promoted Andrew Jackson's programs, such as paying off the national debt, reducing the power of the national bank, and opposing nullification (the right of states to obey some federal laws and not others).

A STRATEGIC MOVE

Andrew Jackson left the presidency in 1837 and was succeeded by Martin Van Buren. Soon after Van Buren took office, the nation plunged into a severe financial crisis called the Panic of 1837. The crisis occurred worldwide and was followed by a long depression, or economic slump. People from all walks

✧ ————————

Martin Van Buren was the eighth president of the United States.

of life suffered tragic losses. Banks closed, businesses failed, and jobs disappeared. Thousands of Americans lost their life savings. Many people became homeless and even suffered from starvation. Women and children haunted city streets begging. The new president called a special session of Congress in September to try to find ways of ending the crisis. However, political factions bickered so much that little could be done.

In Tennessee, Polk's party was having serious problems. People blamed the Democrats for their economic difficulties. They voted for Whigs at local, state, and national levels. The Whig governor of Tennessee, Newton Cannon, was up for reelection in 1839. Tennessee Democrats were desperate to find a candidate who could defeat him. They turned to James Polk as their best possibility and asked him to run for governor.

Polk hesitated. He and Sarah Polk had divided their time between Washington and Tennessee for fourteen years. As Speaker of the House, Polk liked his role at the seat of power. Sarah enjoyed sharing political problems with her husband, and she loved being a popular Washington hostess.

While Polk considered the offer, Andrew Jackson tried to convince Polk that it was his duty to help the failing Democratic Party in Tennessee. Polk didn't want to disappoint Jackson. He was also looking to the future, with hopes of one day serving as vice president of the United States. He knew he would have a higher profile—more fame and name recognition—as a governor than as a congressman. This status would give him a greater chance of being chosen for the national Democratic ticket in 1840.

Nineteenth-Century Orators

In the days before TV, radio, and the Internet, people learned a lot about political issues by listening to politicians speak at public gatherings or by reading their speeches in the newspaper. James K. Polk was an excellent speaker. He presented his arguments in a clear and organized manner. He was often able to convince listeners to accept his point of view.

Other nineteenth-century speakers were even more talented than Polk. The greatest were John C. Calhoun, Daniel Webster, and Henry Clay—all served in the U.S. Congress at some point in their careers. When one of these men spoke in public, thousands gathered to hear him. Hundreds of thousands more rushed out to buy newspapers that printed the speech from beginning to end.

Henry Clay was a gifted speaker, who enthralled his fellow senators during debates on the Senate floor.

John C. Calhoun

Daniel Webster

A southerner, John C. Calhoun was a passionate defender of slavery and states' rights. When he spoke, "there was something that riveted your attention as with hooks of steel," said one listener.

Daniel Webster opposed slavery and efforts by southern states to defy the federal government. Arguing against nullification in 1830, he thundered, "Union and Liberty, now and forever, one and inseparable."

Henry Clay used his flair for making speeches to persuade opposing members of Congress to compromise. Trying to avoid civil war in 1850, he declared in ringing tones: "I implore Senators, by all that is dear to them . . . to look at their country in this crisis—to listen to the voice of reason."

When the congressional session ended, Polk retired from the House. It was customary for House members to honor an outgoing Speaker for his service. They passed a resolution thanking Polk for "the able, impartial, and dignified manner" in which he had presided over the House.

Some of his opponents, however, were angry and bitter. They criticized Polk's efforts as Speaker and noisily opposed the resolution of thanks. Polk rose above this pettiness in a farewell speech to the House. He did not respond to the negative comments but simply pointed out his record of accomplishments. Polk's calm and good-natured response made his opponents look foolish and raised his stature in the eyes of Congress and the nation. Polk returned home to Tennessee to begin his campaign for governor.

REVIVING THE DEMOCRATS

The Democrats of Tennessee rejoiced when James Polk announced he would run for governor. Many Tennessee voters wrote him letters, assuring him of victory. They also urged him to run a campaign based on national issues as well as local ones.

Polk set out upon a series of debates and speeches around Tennessee. He delivered his first speech in Murfreesboro on April 11, 1839. Governor Cannon was invited to speak as well. Polk spoke for two hours, mostly about national issues and the accomplishments of the party of Andrew Jackson. Governor Cannon's response was weak. He was not Polk's equal either in intelligence or speaking ability.

Many more debates followed. Tennessee citizens loved debates. Large crowds gathered to hear the speeches. They cheered their favorite candidate and tossed insults at the other man. Polk was always dignified. He never used vulgar language or insulted his opponent.

Often Polk used the debates to introduce important issues. He believed that citizens in a democracy, in order to make good choices about their government and their leaders, had to be educated and well informed. But few public (government-funded) schools operated in the United States, so Polk proposed a widespread program of free public education. "No people who are not enlightened," he declared, "can long remain free."

Polk's campaign was greatly helped by journalist Jeremiah George Harris, editor of the *Nashville Union.* He wrote many articles supporting Polk and criticizing his opponent.

On Election Day, August 1, 1839, Polk won by less than three thousand votes. Other Democratic candidates also won throughout Tennessee, including majorities in both houses of the state legislature. Although Polk's margin of victory was small, it was still a great personal triumph. His campaign had inspired his party and spurred voters into action. Many men who had never voted before came out on Election Day to cast their votes for Democrats. Some had previously supported Whigs. Polk's arguments persuaded them to switch their party preference.

When the news reached General Jackson, he declared "the return of old democratic Tennessee to the . . . fold again." The new governor-elect, his wife, and other leading Democrats met with the general for a victory celebration that lasted several days.

Polk began his term as governor of Tennessee at the age of forty-three.

CHAPTER FIVE

HOME TO TENNESSEE

He has extraordinary powers of labor,
both mental and physical.
—Andrew Jackson on James Polk

James Polk was inaugurated as governor of Tennessee on October 14, 1839. Andrew Jackson, though aging and unwell, attended the ceremonies at a packed church in Nashville (by then the state capital). In his speech, Polk outlined his plans to improve economic conditions in the state without wasting money. He promised to set down rules for banks that would protect depositors and borrowers, to create and improve schools, and to build public infrastructure such as roads and bridges. He stated his strong belief in local government, saying that "the ultimate and supreme authority rests in the People."

There was no governor's mansion in Tennessee then. The Polks moved into a large brick house on one of the best streets in Nashville. It had pleasant gardens in the rear and spacious rooms where the governor and his wife could receive visitors. Sarah made many friends among the important families of Nashville. The couple received invitations to parties and dinners, but Sarah often had to go alone. Polk, as usual, was working long hours to carry out his new duties.

Becoming governor hurt Polk financially. The campaign had cost a great deal of money. He found himself several thousand dollars in debt. The governor's small salary of two thousand dollars a year did not even pay his living expenses. Polk was forced to borrow more than six thousand dollars and sell some of his property. Fortunately, Polk's plantation in Mississippi was prospering, so he used some of the profits to pay part of his debt each year.

As governor, Polk provided strong leadership for the Democrats and appointed competent people to state government positions. He effectively pulled warring factions together to get things done. He was not able to put all his proposals into action, but he always conducted himself with calmness and dignity. Most important, Polk succeeded in one of his main goals. The chances looked good that a majority of Tennesseans would vote Democratic in the next presidential election.

PLANNING HIS NEXT MOVE

As the 1840 presidential election neared, Polk and his supporters considered the possibility of Polk becoming a candidate for vice president. President Van Buren planned to run for a second term, but he had lost confidence in his current vice president, Colonel Richard M. Johnson. Looking at how James Polk had restored the Democratic

Party to power in Tennessee, party leaders wanted Van Buren to choose Polk as his running mate. Other Democrats also wanted the job, and an intense battle followed for the vice-presidential nomination.

Some of Polk's friends advised him to withdraw from the contest. They said that he was still young, only forty-four, and could run again in the next election. Polk sensed a wind of change in the United States. Many people blamed President Van Buren for the Panic of 1837 and the depression that followed. Polk feared that Van Buren would lose the election. He did not want to be part of a losing ticket, so on June 4, 1840, Polk withdrew his candidacy.

This decision turned out to be wise. Van Buren received a crushing defeat at the polls. The Whig candidate, William Henry Harrison, was elected president of the United States, with John Tyler as his vice president.

———————————— ✧ ————————————

William Henry Harrison (left) *died of pneumonia one month into his presidential term. He was replaced by his vice president, John Tyler* (right).

DOWN BUT NOT OUT

Polk had loyally supported Van Buren during the campaign. This effort worked against him when he ran for governor of Tennessee again in 1841. His Whig opponent, "Slim" Jimmy Jones, was a clever politician. He used crowd-pleasing jokes and sarcasm to make fun of Polk and his support for the unpopular Van Buren. Many Democrats were so discouraged by Van Buren's defeat that they did not bother going to the polls. When the votes were counted, Jones had won by a few thousand votes.

The loss of the election was a blow to Polk. But he told his friends that although he "might be [downcast], he was not destroyed." He assured them that he would continue "battling for the rights of the people."

For the first time in years, James Polk held no political office. He and Sarah took a trip to their plantation in Mississippi. The slow journey and time spent walking about the farm was relaxing and raised Polk's spirits. Then they returned to their family home in Columbia, Tennessee, and Polk resumed his law practice.

He continued to work with the Democratic Party and ran for governor once more in 1843. But in August of that year, Whig candidates received sweeping victories in both state and national elections. James Polk again lost his bid for governor. He was discouraged, yet he couldn't keep away from politics. He again began to think about running for vice president.

Martin Van Buren was certain to be the Democratic candidate for president in 1844. The Whigs were supporting Henry Clay, a popular national figure with experience as a congressman, senator, and secretary of state. The

Democrats knew they would face an uphill battle against Clay in the presidential election. They needed a vice-presidential nominee who would make the ticket stronger.

By then Andrew Jackson was aging and ill. He lay suffering with pain at the Hermitage, his home near Nashville, but he was still the leader of the Democratic Party. Despite his pain, he continued to work on strategies for achieving victory. In September 1843, Jackson wrote a letter to the *Nashville Union* stating that Van Buren's election would be assured if Polk's name were added to the ticket. The editors of the newspaper agreed. They declared Polk to be "one of the ablest men in the democratic party in the southwest."

———————— ✧ ————————

Andrew Jackson's home in Tennessee, the Hermitage, opened as a museum in 1889.

Other Democratic leaders in Tennessee took up Polk's cause. Messages traveled across the state and nation urging his nomination. The Democratic National Convention was scheduled to meet in the spring of 1844. Polk's nomination was far from assured, however. Some factions in the party supported other candidates. Most agreed that Van Buren was their choice for the top spot on the ticket. Then the question of Texas arose and caused chaos within the party.

TURMOIL OVER TEXAS

In the 1840s, many Americans from the East Coast were traveling westward, setting up farms and towns on the frontier. Many of them settled in Texas, which had rebelled against Mexico and become an independent republic in 1836. As newcomers settled more and more western lands, some Americans claimed that the United States had a "manifest destiny" (an inevitable fate) to spread across the continent from the Atlantic Ocean to the Pacific Ocean.

Many leaders wanted to annex Texas to the United States (add it as a new U.S. territory). But the idea was dangerous. It could lead to war with Mexico, since that country still claimed Texas as its own. Furthermore, the fact that Texas permitted slavery created divisions between anti-slavery northerners and proslavery southerners.

Reporters asked all the presidential and vice-presidential candidates to state their opinions on the annexation of Texas. Polk said he favored annexation. Van Buren, however, declared that he opposed slavery and didn't want to see another slaveholding territory enter the Union.

Many Democrats, including Andrew Jackson, were furious with Van Buren. Most Americans strongly favored the

This painting symbolically represents the idea of manifest destiny. The angel figure represents the United States and leads pioneers and railroads westward.

─────── ✧ ───────

annexation of Texas. Supporting annexation could assure a Democratic victory, since their Whig opponent, Henry Clay, opposed it. Van Buren's stand created a serious problem for the Democrats.

Andrew Jackson had been a firm supporter of Martin Van Buren. But he believed even more strongly in the policy of manifest destiny and the importance of annexing Texas. He decided that the Democratic Party must nominate a different candidate for president: someone who supported annexation.

Lewis and Clark (center) *on their cross-country expedition*

———————— ✧ ————————

THE EXPANSIONIST VISION

After the American Revolution, the United States was a nation of thirteen states, all on the East Coast. As the years passed, however, the East became more and more crowded. To find more land and business opportunities, people moved west. Scouts such as Daniel Boone crossed the Appalachian Mountains. They discovered the rich lands of Tennessee and Kentucky. Settlers followed and then began to look even farther westward. They dreamed of an expanding nation.

Thomas Jefferson was one of these dreamers. As president, he carried out the Louisiana Purchase in 1803. He bought almost 900,000 square miles of land from France for only $15 million. The land stretched from the Mississippi River to the Rocky Mountains. This purchase almost doubled the size of the United States. Jefferson sent an expedition, headed by army officers Meriwether Lewis and William Clark, to explore the new territory. They traveled along rivers, over mountains, and through forests to map the wilderness.

Thousands of settlers and adventurers followed the path set by Lewis and Clark. They wanted to make new homes and farms in the vast western lands. In doing so, they encountered Native Americans, whose ancestors had occupied North America for generations. The Native Americans battled to keep white settlers from taking over their traditional lands. But the powerful U.S. Army was too strong for them. White troops killed thousands of Native Americans. The survivors were forced onto reservations, where their freedoms were greatly restricted.

Most white Americans did not question the takeover of Native American lands. They believed it was God's will for the United States to spread from the Atlantic to the Pacific Ocean—an idea called manifest destiny.

A few weeks before the National Democratic Convention, Jackson invited Polk to a meeting at the Hermitage. At the meeting, Polk reported, General Jackson expressed "the opinion that I would be the most available man." A few days later, Jackson published a letter in the *Nashville Union*, clearly suggesting that Texas had to be annexed and Van Buren had to be dropped as the Democratic presidential nominee. This letter changed everything for James Polk. His ambition had been to become vice president of the United States. All of a sudden, the strongest voice in the Democratic Party wanted him to be the candidate for president. Van Buren's supporters, however, held fast to their candidate.

THE DARK HORSE

James Polk was home in Tennessee when the Democratic National Convention met in Baltimore, Maryland, on May 27, 1844. Delegates were welcomed by the booming sound of two cannons captured from the British during the American Revolution. The noise inside the hall was even more deafening. Delegates (state representatives who elect the presidential nominee) kept shouting to be heard, as the chairman's gavel banged for order.

The party seemed hopelessly divided between anti-annexation delegates—backing Van Buren—and pro-annexation delegates, who backed other candidates. The convention rules stated that a candidate had to receive two-thirds of the vote to win the nomination. During the next two days, the delegates voted seven times. But each time, no candidate received enough votes to win. The convention was deadlocked.

A flurry of private meetings followed. Obviously, Van Buren's cause was hopeless. The Democrats needed to find a candidate who could unite the party. This candidate had to favor annexation, since this position gave the Democrats an advantage over Henry Clay. The candidate also had to be able to carry both the North (mostly against annexation) and the South, which supported it.

George Bancroft, who led the Massachusetts delegation, pointed out that James Polk of Tennessee met all these requirements. His years as a hardworking congressman and Speaker of the House had brought him approval from northerners as well as southerners. He had executive (head-of-government) experience as governor of Tennessee. He was pro-annexation and had the support of Andrew Jackson, who was still immensely popular with the American people. Bancroft set to work to convince the other delegates to back Polk.

✧ ————————

George Bancroft suggested Polk as the Democratic presidential candidate in the 1844 election.

On the morning of the third day of the convention, a delegate nominated James Polk as a compromise candidate. The delegates voted an eighth time. Some delegates switched their votes to Polk, but not enough to win him a two-thirds majority. Then, on the ninth ballot, more delegates threw their support to Polk. A delegate from Pennsylvania, initially a Van Buren supporter, explained his decision to switch, calling Polk "the . . . friend of General Jackson, and a pure, whole-hogged democrat, the known enemy of banks." State after state rushed to add their votes to the final tally. A large majority nominated James Polk for president and George M. Dallas for vice president.

At home in Tennessee, James Polk was shocked when a messenger handed him a note stating that he had won the presidential nomination. In horse racing, the term *dark horse* refers to a horse that is not well known and is unlikely to win. The term was used for the first time in political history to describe the candidacy of James K. Polk.

CHAPTER SIX

ROAD TO THE WHITE HOUSE

Who is James K. Polk?
—1844 Whig campaign slogan

The Democrats united behind Polk, whom they nicknamed Young Hickory to emphasize his relationship to Old Hickory. But defeating their Whig opponent, Henry Clay, would not be easy. Clay had been a force in politics for many decades. He was famous throughout the United States and much admired for his skill as a speaker. The Whigs immediately adopted a slogan to ridicule Polk, who was unknown to most Americans. "Who is James K. Polk?" they asked.

The Democrats came up with a slogan of their own. "Fifty-Four Forty or Fight!" they trumpeted. This slogan referred to 54 degrees, 40 minutes north latitude (54°40'), a line on the map running through northern Canada. As part of their campaign platform (the party's positions on issues), Democrats said that the United States should

This campaign banner was made for Polk and his running mate George M. Dallas in the 1844 presidential election.
✧ ————————————

acquire all of Oregon Country (the Pacific Northwest) up to this line, even though Great Britain also claimed the land. Their platform also included cutting the cost of running the government, lowering taxes and tariffs, and the annexation of Texas.

DIRTY TRICKS

At that time, presidential nominees did not go on the campaign trail making speeches. They were expected to follow the example of the first president, George Washington, who thought it was beneath the dignity of a president to campaign. Instead, each candidate's supporters traveled around the country, trying to convince people to vote for their man. Polk and Clay were active behind the scenes, however. They organized the campaigns and wrote letters to newspapers and influential citizens. Sarah Polk worked as her husband's personal secretary and chief adviser. She helped plan campaign activities and wrote letters.

As time went on, the arguments became more personal and insulting. Clay's supporters called Polk names and spread lies about him. Newspaper articles claimed that his grandfather had been a Tory (supporter of the British) during the American Revolution. Another story accused Polk of mistreating the slaves on his plantations. None of these stories was true. Clay's backers even attacked Sarah Polk. They said that her lack of children made her unsuitable as a First Lady.

Democrats responded in kind. They pointed out that Henry Clay used vulgar language. They called him a drunkard, a gambler, and a liar.

THE FINAL TALLY

Voting began on November 1 in Pennsylvania and Ohio. Election Day occurred later in other states, so from start to finish, the presidential election lasted nearly two weeks. As the votes were being counted, Polk remained home in Columbia, Tennessee.

In the U.S. Electoral College system, each state is allotted a certain number of electoral votes, according to its size. The candidate who wins the most popular votes in a state receives all of that state's electoral votes. The candidate with the most electoral votes wins.

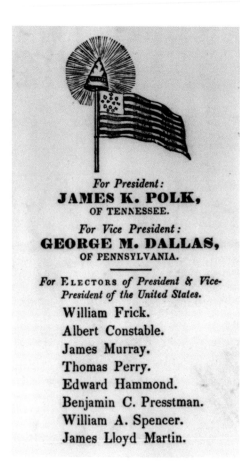

For President:
JAMES K. POLK,
OF TENNESSEE.

For Vice President:
GEORGE M. DALLAS,
OF PENNSYLVANIA.

For E LECTORS *of President & Vice-President of the United States.*

William Frick.
Albert Constable.
James Murray.
Thomas Perry.
Edward Hammond.
Benjamin C. Presstman.
William A. Spencer.
James Lloyd Martin.

This Democratic election ticket for the 1844 presidential campaign shows the names of the party's eight electors for the state of Maryland.

On the night of November 14, the mail train from New York arrived in Nashville at 9 P.M. The postmaster saw a note that had been scrawled on the outside of a package by another postmaster down the line. Polk had won! The Nashville postmaster, General Robert Armstrong, grinned. He was a good friend of the Polks. He quickly sent a messenger to their home in Columbia, Tennessee. In this way, James Polk learned the results of the election before the news was made public. He had received 170 electoral votes to Clay's 105. He and Sarah were jubilant.

Their first celebration was private, just between themselves. They said nothing about the victory to their friends and neighbors. Polk went about his work quietly for twenty-four hours. During that day, friends expressed sympathy. They felt that such a long delay in getting the election results meant that Polk had been defeated. Polk's face was expressionless. He kept the big news to himself. Very soon, however, the results became public. "Who is J. K. Polk will be no more asked," Andrew Jackson declared when he heard about Polk's victory.

Before leaving for Washington to begin his term as president, Polk spent three days at the Hermitage. There, he conferred with Andrew Jackson and other Democratic leaders. The new administration had many problems to iron out. One was the split in the Democratic Party. Martin Van Buren had many followers. They were still angry that Polk had replaced him on the ticket. Polk and Jackson talked about how to make peace with the Van Buren Democrats.

Polk left the meeting at the Hermitage optimistic about his new job. He had heaviness in his heart too. Seventy-eight-year-old Andrew Jackson was frail and weak. But the two friends parted with promises to write each other often.

BACK TO WASHINGTON

On a cold February morning, James and Sarah Polk set out for Washington, D.C. Their journey began on a river ship called the *China,* which sailed from a wharf on the Cumberland River in Nashville. Thousands of people thronged Nashville's Broad Street, cheering as the ship nosed into the current. Not long into the journey, on the Ohio River, the *China* ran into a raging storm. The river waters turned into foaming whirlpools. The ship was tossed about helplessly. Wood splintered and windows shattered. Finally, the *China* was blown ashore and came to rest against a tree. Fortunately, no one was injured, and the ship was soon under way again.

The Polks stepped off the ship at several landing stages along the river. Large, admiring crowds met them at each stop. The president-elect and his wife listened politely to many speeches wishing them success.

The boat trip ended at Wheeling, Virginia (now West Virginia). From there, the new first couple traveled across the mountains in a luxurious horse-drawn coach especially made for the occasion. It was painted green and lined with red silk. Emblazoned in gold on the door were the words *The President.* They left the coach at Cumberland, Maryland, and rode the rest of the way on a steam-powered railroad train. As they neared Washington, an operator blew the steam engine's whistle at full blast. A roar of cannons answered it from Capitol Hill. The president-elect was then greeted by the U.S. Marine Band playing "Hail to the Chief."

"THE TRUE-BLUE DEMOCRACY"

James K. Polk was inaugurated the eleventh president of the United States on March 4, 1845. He was forty-nine years old, then the youngest man ever elected president.

A large crowd gathered to watch him take the oath of office outside the U.S. Capitol. Sarah Polk sat proudly in the visitor's gallery. She wore a red-and-gray-striped silk dress, a beige cape, and a red velvet bonnet. She held a beautiful ivory fan decorated with pictures of all the eleven U.S. presidents, including her husband. Rain fell in torrents as the visitors waited for the new president to begin his inaugural address. According to attendee John Quincy Adams, Polk had to speak to "a large assemblage of umbrellas."

In his speech, President Polk spoke about the principles that were important to him. He defined the ideal government as one that lived within its means and did not get into debt. He warned about the danger of dividing the country over the angry debate on slavery and emphasized that preserving the Union should always be the primary

This commemorative print was published after the inauguration of Polk. It includes a portrait of each of the eleven presidents, with Washington in the center and Polk at the bottom.

---- ◇ ----

goal. He said he opposed bringing back a national bank, and he proposed a tariff to raise money for the country.

He said he believed that expansion was good for the country. In ringing words, he declared that by extending the country's borders, "the bonds of our Union, so far from

being weakened, will become stronger." He specifically discussed Oregon and stated that the United States had an
unquestionable right to the land.

At the end of the thirty-minute speech, Polk pledged
that he would do what was best for the country, not just
one political party. His speech was well received. Even people
who had opposed him were impressed by his words.

The Polks were honored that evening with two inaugural
balls. One cost ten dollars a ticket and was open to all.
The other, for Democrats only, cost five dollars a ticket.
The Polks made an appearance at both celebrations. Sarah
wore a powder blue silk dress with a floral design woven
into the material. The couple did not dance at either
party, since Sarah was a strict Presbyterian, and her faith
frowned upon dancing. But the couple had their dinner
at the Democrats-only party, called the "the true-blue five-
dollar Democracy" by one observer.

CHAPTER SEVEN

THE POLK PRESIDENCY

*I am the hardest working man
in this country.*
—President James Polk

One of James Polk's first jobs upon taking the office of president was to choose his cabinet, his group of five top advisers. In choosing, Polk tried to be fair to all wings of the party. He also wanted different parts of the country represented in his cabinet: two of the men were from the North, the other three were southerners. They were all experienced politicians. Even one of Polk's critics commented that his cabinet was "one of the ablest ever assembled around any executive."

In addition to the cabinet, Polk had to choose people to fill less important government positions. Immediately, an army of visitors besieged him, all of them asking for jobs. "I am utterly disgusted with the constant . . . press for office with which I have been annoyed," Polk wrote.

This photograph of Polk and his cabinet in 1849 is the first photo of a president and his cabinet, as well as the first interior photograph of the White House.

Many job seekers were disappointed. The new president was determined to appoint only people who had proper qualifications and ability. Some of the office seekers he turned away became his enemies, but most observers supported his independence and fairness.

For the nation as a whole, Polk came into office with four goals to accomplish in just one term. First, he wanted to pass a low tariff that would be acceptable to people in industry and agriculture in all parts of the country, both North and South. Next, he planned to establish an independent treasury, a government banking system (but quite different from the Bank of the United States) that would help bring order to the nation's financial situation. He also vowed to settle the dispute with Great Britain over Oregon Country and set the northwestern boundaries of the United States. Finally, he hoped to acquire California and establish a country that stretched from one end of the continent to the other.

Texas was not mentioned in this list of goals. Congress had already approved the annexation of Texas during the final days of the previous administration. Problems remained, however. Mexico still claimed Texas and threatened to seize the territory by war if necessary.

Polk and Andrew Jackson kept the promise they had made at the Hermitage to write to each other regularly. Young Hickory asked for advice. Old Hickory gave it freely. The time came, however, when Jackson was so weak that he could barely lift a pen. On June 6, 1845, he sent his final letter to the new president. The writing was shaky, and the paper filled with blots of ink. "I can write no more," he concluded. "Friendship has roused me to make this attempt." Four days later, Andrew Jackson was dead. The entire nation mourned the passing of the great leader, none more so than his friend and protégé, James Polk.

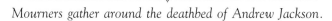

Mourners gather around the deathbed of Andrew Jackson.

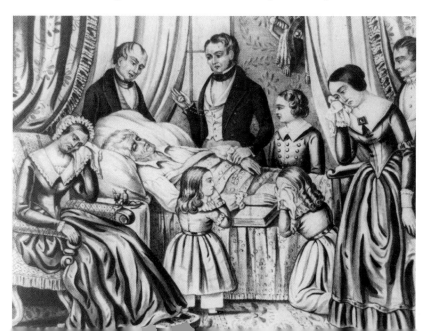

Sarah Polk, First Lady

One of President Polk's chief assets during his years in the White House was his wife, Sarah Polk (*below*). She watched over her husband's health and gave him emotional support. She countered his seriousness with her own personal charm and sociability.

Sarah acted as her husband's secretary and adviser. Often Polk would hand his wife a pack of daily newspapers. She studied them for him and clipped items she thought he should see. She also saved his time by choosing certain books and articles for him to read.

Women then were not supposed to show an interest in politics—after all, only men could vote and hold political office. But Sarah had definite political opinions. She expressed them freely in private with small groups of friends or political allies. But in keeping with the customs of the time, she underplayed her political interests in public.

As First Lady, Sarah was the White House hostess. She organized public receptions and planned elegant weekly dinners for thirty or more people. Sarah invited Polk's political enemies to many of these events. By seeing them socially, the Polks could discover their opponents' thoughts and plans.

Because of her religious beliefs, Sarah refused to allow dancing, card playing, or liquor at the White House. Still, Sarah was a popular hostess. The press loved to write about her parties and receptions. She hosted the first annual Thanksgiving dinner at the White House. She also saw to it that the White House operated economically. The government gave her fifty thousand dollars a year to run the household, but she spent less than half of it.

Gaslights—the newest, most modern type of lighting at the time—were installed at the White House during Polk's presidency. Despite the new lights, Sarah insisted on keeping the old candle chandelier in the Blue Room, and she received much teasing about it. The teasing stopped when the gaslights failed during a state reception. Thanks to Sarah's planning, the party was able to continue in the candle-lit Blue Room.

President James K. Polk
———————— ◆ ————————

THE HARDWORKING PRESIDENT

James Polk approached the duties of a president in the same way he had tackled every previous job. He kept a rigid schedule in the White House, getting up at dawn, breakfasting early, and working nonstop until five o'clock. After dining and attending to any social obligations (parties or receptions), he returned to work.

He pored over books and papers to become familiar with all departments in his branch of government. "The President . . . signs nothing without the strictest examination," wrote one observer, "and has frequently, to the confusion of clerks, detected serious errors in the papers sent for his signature." Often his labors went on far into the night. "No president who performs his duties faithfully and conscientiously can have any leisure," he wrote.

Polk had firm ideas about right and wrong. He received many gifts, but he returned almost all of them—lest the gift giver expect a political favor from him in exchange. One supporter sent him a case of expensive wines and imported foods. Polk instructed the man to send him a bill for the goods or to take them away. Eventually, colleagues understood that the president would accept nothing of greater value than a book or a cane.

Secretary of State James Buchanan suggested that Polk keep a diary of his time in office. Polk began the diary in August 1845 and made entries in it faithfully throughout his presidency. He expressed his opinions on every issue and wrote down the events of each day in great detail.

———————————— ✧ ————————————

Polk wrote in his diary every day of his presidency. This particular entry is about his last day in office.

POLK AND SLAVERY

Like many southerners, James Polk was a slave owner. He and Sarah owned several household slaves, as well as slaves who worked on their plantations. On one hand, Polk thought that slave labor was important to the economy of the South. He and other plantation owners thought that their large farms could not make money without slave labor. On the other hand, Polk realized that slavery was brutal and immoral. He believed that the practice would eventually die out on its own. In his will, James Polk ordered that all his slaves should be freed after the death of his wife.

The debate over slavery increased during the 1840s, when several new territories and states were joining the Union. Many northerners wanted to make slavery illegal in the new territories and states. Southerners insisted that slavery be permitted there.

As president, James Polk tried to remain neutral in the slavery debate. He usually kept his thoughts on the issue to himself and tried to tone down the dispute. Neither side appreciated his efforts, however. Northerners denounced him as a slave owner, and southerners criticized him because he did not speak in defense of slavery.

Neither Polk nor the presidents who followed him could keep slavery from tearing the nation apart. The issue finally came to a head in 1861, when eleven southern states withdrew from the Union, leading to the outbreak of the Civil War (1861–1865).

OREGON COUNTRY

In Polk's first diary entry, August 26, 1845, he set down his plans for Oregon. The United States and Great Britain had managed the disputed territory jointly since signing a treaty in 1818. Both British and U.S. citizens lived and worked in the region. The British had business interests there, including a profitable fur trade.

But U.S. leaders considered Oregon a perfect place to enact their policy of manifest destiny. The territory was rich and fertile. Thousands of settlers had journeyed across the continent to make new homes in Oregon's Columbia River valley. To Polk and other U.S. leaders, it seemed only right that this entire territory should belong to the United States.

✧ ———————

This map shows the area in the Pacific Northwest that was managed jointly by the United States and Great Britain in the mid-1800s.

Polk hoped that the British would agree to give up part of the territory to the United States. But he realized that the campaign goal of 54°40' was unrealistic. It would bring the U.S. border deep into northern Canada—Polk knew the British would never agree to give up so much land.

Polk directed Secretary of State Buchanan to write a letter to Sir Richard Pakenham, Britain's representative in Washington. In the letter, Buchanan suggested a compromise plan, setting the northern U.S. border at latitude 49 (also called the 49th parallel). This dividing line made sense because it matched the northern U.S. border farther

✧ ————————————

James Buchanan served as Polk's secretary of state.

east. But Pakenham rejected the offer. The attempt at compromise had failed. Months passed. Both Great Britain and the United States began to build forts and arm settlers in the territory, preparing to settle the dispute by war.

In December 1845, Polk delivered the president's annual message to Congress. In it he restated his intention to obtain Oregon for the United States. To support his position, Polk cited the Monroe Doctrine. This policy, established in 1823 by President James Monroe, stated that no foreign power would be permitted to establish a colony in the Americas. Polk insisted that this doctrine meant that Great Britain did not have a lawful claim to Oregon. He pointed out that efforts at compromise had failed. It was up to Congress, he told them, to decide on the next move.

A furious debate followed. Some congressmen insisted on holding out for 54°40', even if it meant going to war. Others supported compromise. The president urged Congress to be firm. "The only way to treat John Bull [Britain]," he insisted, "[is] to look him straight in the eyes." In April 1846, both houses of Congress—the Senate and the House of Representatives—passed a resolution ending the joint administration of Oregon with Great Britain. The president signed it immediately.

British leaders knew that the numbers of U.S. settlers in Oregon were increasing and that Americans outnumbered British citizens there. They also realized that as U.S. settlements grew, wilderness areas would shrink, and their North American fur trade would decline and eventually end. With the threat of war looming, the British reconsidered their stance on Oregon. They offered a compromise much like the one they had rejected earlier, agreeing to divide Oregon at the 49th parallel.

The United States accepted the offer. It gained the land that would become the states of Washington, Idaho, and Oregon. The British received Vancouver Island (north of Seattle) and all of western Canada above the 49th parallel. The U.S. Senate ratified the Oregon Treaty in June 1846.

KEEPING HIS PROMISES

James Polk had accomplished one of his most important objectives with the Oregon Treaty. In August 1846, he achieved a second goal by signing a law that sharply reduced tariffs on imported goods. Even though this law angered some northern industrialists, it had a positive effect on the U.S. economy. The new law encouraged free trade (the exchange of goods) between countries. Britain responded favorably by allowing foreign countries to sell grain in Great Britain. Farmers in the western United States benefited from this new market.

Polk's third pledge was to establish an independent treasury. This would be a nationwide system of public banks that would hold and regulate government funds. The new treasury would take government money out of the hands of private bankers, who often put their own interests before the good of the nation. But it wouldn't be too powerful or poorly managed, like the old Bank of the United States that Andrew Jackson had shut down. Congress approved the independent treasury in 1846.

Polk's fourth goal was to obtain California from Mexico. To build up U.S. influence in the region, he encouraged

Kit Carson stands with his friend John C. Frémont.

✧ ————————

farmers and businesspeople to settle there. He also sent an expedition—headed by John C. Frémont and guided by soldier and scout Kit Carson—to explore California. By acquiring California, the United States could fulfill its manifest destiny—extending the nation all the way to the Pacific Ocean.

U.S. soldiers storm Monterrey, Mexico, during the
Mexican-American War (1846–1848).

CHAPTER EIGHT

WAR WITH MEXICO

I shall regard Texas as a part of the Union. . . . We should not stand quietly by and permit an invading foreign enemy to occupy . . . any portion of Texas territory.

—James Polk

When Texas first became part of the United States, it was not a state but a territory (a region with limited self-government). Immediately afterward, Texans began a movement to bring their territory into the Union as a state. Antislavery forces were angry. Slavery was legal in Texas, and opponents of slavery did not want the nation to accept another slave state. After bitter debate, Congress passed an act admitting Texas to the Union as the twenty-eighth state. President Polk signed the measure on December 29, 1845.

The Mexican government was furious. It had never recognized Texas's independence, and it opposed Texas joining the United States. In addition, Mexico and the

United States disputed Texas's southern border. Mexico claimed that the boundary was the Nueces River. The United States said it was the Rio Grande, about 150 miles south of the Nueces.

Immediately after Texas won its statehood, the Mexican government broke off friendly relations with the United States. Mexican armies began to mass along the Rio Grande. President Polk wrote to General Sam Houston, a leading political figure in Texas. He assured Houston that the U.S. government would protect Texas against Mexico.

Polk sent forces under General Zachary Taylor to the Nueces River. He also ordered Robert Stockton, commander of the Pacific Squadron of the U.S. Navy—stationed off the California coast—to stand by. He told the commander to be ready to seize California in the event of war with Mexico.

A STATE OF WAR

The cries for war grew louder in both the United States and Mexico. Early in 1846, Polk ordered General Taylor to move his army to the north bank of the Rio Grande. This

✧ ————————————
General Sam Houston

General Zachary Taylor

was the border between Texas and Mexico as claimed by the United States. The town of Matamoros lay directly across the river. It was filled with Mexican troops.

In April 1846, the Mexican general in Matamoros sent a message to Taylor. He demanded that Taylor take his men back to the Nueces—the river that Mexico considered to be the Texas-Mexico border. General Taylor refused. On April 26, 1,600 Mexican soldiers crossed the Rio Grande. They came upon a U.S. Army scouting party of 63 cavalrymen (soldiers on horseback). The large Mexican force surrounded them. They killed and wounded many of the U.S. troops and took the rest prisoner.

President Polk had been preparing a message to Congress. In it he planned to ask for a declaration of war against Mexico. When word reached him about the attack on the U.S. cavalry scouts, Polk changed his message: He accused Mexico of invading U.S. territory. "Mexico has passed the boundary of the United States . . . and shed American blood upon American soil," Polk stated. It was no longer necessary to declare war, he said. A state of war already existed.

On May 11, 1846, Congress voted to declare war on Mexico. The vote passed by a large majority, with only a few congressmen voting no. One was a young Whig congressman, Abraham Lincoln. He criticized Polk, saying, "[T]he war with Mexico was unnecessarily and unconstitutionally [begun] by the President."

THE COMMANDER IN CHIEF TAKES CHARGE

When the war began, the regular U.S. Army numbered only seven thousand troops—much smaller than the Mexican force of thirty-two thousand men. Polk called up volunteer regiments to increase the number of U.S. troops. The main U.S. force invaded Mexico in August 1846. The president also sent troops to New Mexico and California.

In New Mexico, Mexican armies melted under an attack led by Brigadier General Stephen Kearny. In California, Polk ordered a combined invasion. Captain John C. Frémont attacked by land. Meanwhile, Robert Stockton's naval forces invaded from the sea. By January 1847, the conquest of California was complete.

Despite having capable generals at his command—many of them recent graduates of the U.S. Military Academy at West Point, New York—Polk did not rely upon his officers. From the beginning, he took personal command, supervising the conduct of the war in every detail. Entries from his diary show how deeply he was involved. "I expressed . . . my dissatisfaction," he wrote on August 29, 1846, "at the delay . . . in the departure of Col. Stephenson's Regiment in New York, destined for California. I directed the Secretary to have them . . . sent off with the least possible delay." On the same day, he noted, "I suggested the importance of taking Vera Cruz by a land force to be landed out of reach of the fortress . . . and by cooperating with the blockading squadron by sea."

President Polk proved to be a skilled commander in chief, and the war in Mexico went well. At home, however, political problems plagued the president. Abolitionists saw the war as a plot to add slave states such as Texas to the Union. They stepped up their opposition to Polk and the war.

VICTORY!

In the fall of 1846, General Taylor crossed the Rio Grande and captured Monterrey, Mexico. This victory gave U.S. forces control of northeastern Mexico. The newspapers called Taylor a great hero, nicknaming him Old Rough and Ready. His popularity soared. His supporters immediately began a campaign to make him a presidential nominee in the next election.

In February 1847, Polk directed General Taylor to move

toward Mexico City from the north. First, Taylor defeated the Mexican army at the town of Buena Vista. Meanwhile, General Winfield Scott landed

✧ ————————————
General Winfield Scott

Following Polk's directions, U.S. forces land at Veracruz, Mexico, in 1847 under the command of General Scott.

his forces at the port of Veracruz on the Gulf of Mexico. Mexico City was caught between the two invading forces. Scott finally captured it in September 1847.

The president sent a member of the State Department to discuss surrender with Mexican general Antonio López de Santa Anna. At first, Santa Anna refused to surrender. Some U.S. leaders, such as Secretary of State James Buchanan, began to talk about taking over all of Mexico. But Polk ignored this suggestion and continued to negotiate with Santa Anna.

In February 1848, the Mexicans accepted Polk's peace terms. Later that year, the two nations signed the Treaty of Guadalupe Hidalgo. It fixed the border between Mexico and the United States at the Rio Grande. The

BUILDINGS AND INSTITUTIONS

Several famous U.S. landmarks and organizations took root during the Polk administration. First, President Polk helped set up a school to train officers for the U.S. Navy. He worked on this project with George Bancroft, secretary of the navy. Opened in August 1845 in Annapolis, Maryland, the institution was first called the Naval School. It was renamed the U.S. Naval Academy in 1850.

In 1846 Polk attended ceremonies for the beginning of construction on the Smithsonian Institution in Washington, D.C. Founded with a gift of $500,000 from British scientist James Smithson, the Smithsonian eventually grew to become the largest museum complex in the world and a major research and educational center.

On July 4, 1848, President Polk laid the cornerstone for the Washington Monument. The monument, standing 555 feet high, honors George Washington, the first president of the United States.

treaty also made Mexico give up the present-day states of California, Nevada, and Utah, and parts of present-day Arizona, Colorado, Wyoming, and New Mexico. The United States paid Mexico $15 million for the land.

With the treaty, the United States grew by more than 500,000 square miles. James Polk had achieved all the goals he had set out for his presidency.

CHAPTER NINE

FINAL DAYS

This day closes my third year in the presidential office. They have been years of . . . labor and anxiety.
—James Polk's diary entry, March 3, 1848

James Polk neared the end of his presidency with great relief. He was proud of his record. He had accomplished everything he had promised to do. But he had worked extremely hard, and his health had begun to suffer. He looked far older than his fifty-three years. People who saw him at the end of his term commented on his "haggard look [and] flowing gray locks."

From the beginning of his presidency, Polk had insisted that he would serve only one term. Friends and supporters tried to change his mind. They urged him to accept the Democratic nomination in 1848. They pointed out how deeply split the party had become over the slavery issue and said that Polk was the only one who could

THE DEMOCRATIC FUNERAL OF 1848.

*This cartoon predicts a political death for the
Democrats in the election of 1848.*

reunite it. Without him, they insisted, the party would lose the presidency.

But Polk made his future plans clear in a letter to the Democratic National Convention. His only desire, he said, was "to retire to private life at the close of my present term." He planned to spend his retirement at Polk Place, a house he and Sarah owned in Nashville.

With Polk out of the running, the Democrats chose Lewis Cass, a senator from Michigan, as their candidate for president. He was not well known and seemed unlikely to win the race. His opponents were Martin Van Buren, running with a new antislavery party called the Free Soilers, and General Zachary Taylor, running as a Whig. A popular war hero, Taylor easily won the 1848 election.

The Polks traveled to New Orleans, Louisiana, by steamboat in 1849.

———————— ✧ ————————

A BRIEF RETIREMENT

On March 5, 1849, the day after Taylor's inauguration, President Polk and his wife braved an icy rain to begin their journey home. The Polks did not go directly home to Tennessee. First, they took a long journey through the South, where Polk had many supporters.

The couple's first stop was Richmond, Virginia, where Polk spoke to the state's House of Delegates. The Polks continued south, making stops in the Carolinas and Georgia. Everywhere, bands and cheering crowds greeted them. In Mobile, Alabama, they boarded a steamboat for New Orleans. There, crowds lined the streets as the Polks drove past in an open carriage. They enjoyed an elaborate dinner in their honor, with hundreds of guests attending.

Soon afterward, Polk became ill. He grew extremely weak and suffered from severe stomach pains. Sarah heard about an outbreak of cholera (a sometimes deadly disease) in New Orleans, and she feared the worst. Despite Polk's illness, the couple continued on to Memphis, Tennessee, where a doctor advised Polk to rest.

After a few days, he rallied enough to travel the final leg of the journey to Nashville. A huge crowd was waiting on the dock to greet him and Sarah. It had been a grueling month since their departure from Washington.

Polk began to recover in the peace and quiet of Polk Place. After a few weeks, he felt well enough to begin lining the shelves of his library with books. But then his health worsened. In June doctors confirmed that he indeed had cholera. As Sarah feared, he had caught it in New Orleans.

Doctors had little hope that Polk would recover. Polk called for a minister, who baptized him into the church—a baptism that had been postponed since his infancy. A few days later, on June 15, 1849, James Polk died of cholera. He was fifty-three years old and had left the presidency only three months earlier. He was buried at Polk Place. (In 1893 his remains were moved to the grounds of the Tennessee Capitol in Nashville.)

SARAH AT POLK PLACE

Sarah Polk lived alone at Polk Place for forty-two more years. She never remarried, and she devoted herself to keeping her husband's memory alive. She kept everything in his study exactly as he had left it on the day of his death. His books still lined the walls. His writing papers and pens still lay on the table. Every document, including his diary, was carefully preserved. No hand but Sarah's was permitted to dust them.

POLK MEMORIAL SITES

People who want to learn more about James Polk can get firsthand information by visiting two of his homes. The first, the Polk Memorial, is in Mecklenburg County, North Carolina, on land once owned by James Polk's parents. James spent the first eleven years of his life there.

Polk's boyhood home is no longer standing, but visitors to the site can tour a similar log home, a freestanding kitchen, and a barn, all dating from the period of Polk's childhood. All the furnishings and equipment in the buildings also date from the early 1800s.

Exhibits at the site commemorate important events of Polk's presidency, such as the Mexican War, the Oregon boundary dispute, and the annexation of California. Visitors can also watch a film about James K. Polk there.

Another Polk home, the James K. Polk Ancestral Home in Columbia, Tennessee, is a Federal-style brick home. Except for the White House, it is the only home where James Polk once lived that still survives. Polk's father built the house in 1816,

The James K. Polk Ancestral Home in Columbia, Tennessee, has a fan-shaped window over the front door—one of the hallmarks of the Federal style.

while the future president was attending the University of North Carolina. Polk lived with his parents in this house when he was first practicing law and beginning his political career. In 1824 he married Sarah Childress, and they moved into a house of their own.

The ancestral home contains many original Polk family items, including furniture and paintings. Also on display are china settings used in the White House during Polk's presidency and a cast-iron fountain from Polk Place, which burned down in 1900. The site also features a museum where visitors can watch a video about Polk, view photographs of James and Sarah Polk, and see artifacts such as the fan Sarah Polk carried on Inauguration Day.

For a few years after her husband's death, Sarah seemed to retreat from the world. She dressed only in black and saw few people. Gradually, she became more active and began to receive visitors from Tennessee and around the nation. She took in an orphaned grandniece and brought her up as her own child.

During the Civil War, Sarah declared Polk Place to be neutral ground—even though war raged all around her. Sarah graciously received visitors from both sides of the conflict, although she herself sympathized with the South.

Sarah Childress Polk died at Polk Place in 1891 at the age of eighty-seven. She was buried next to her husband on the grounds of the Tennessee Capitol.

PRESIDENTIAL LEGACY

James Polk's dedication and steady labor brought him many successes and admirers, but he was never a popular president. He spent little time polishing his public image. Many people saw him as too stern and serious. Some newspapers sneeringly called him Tom Thumb—an insulting reference to his short stature (Tom Thumb was a famous person of unusually small size). Within his own party, proslavery and antislavery Democrats often blamed Polk for not siding with one group or the other. After his death, some criticized Polk for failing to take a stand on slavery and for his eagerness to go to war with Mexico.

For almost a century, historians ignored Polk's accomplishments. He was dismissed as an unimportant president. In recent years, however, historians have taken another look at James K. Polk. Many consider Polk to be the only strong president between Andrew Jackson and Abraham

Lincoln. He was able to carry out every one of his campaign promises. He planned and oversaw a victorious war with Mexico. He expanded the nation's borders west to the Pacific Ocean and north to the 49th parallel. He practiced the ideals put forth by Andrew Jackson, including the belief that "the President is the direct representative of the American people."

Some modern historians are beginning to include Polk on the list of "great presidents." Others call him "near great." Harry Truman, thirty-third president of the United States, admired Polk tremendously, calling him simply: "A great president [who] said what he intended to do and did it."

TIMELINE

1795 James K. Polk is born on November 2 in Mecklenburg County, North Carolina.

1806 The Polk family moves to Duck River valley in Tennessee.

1812 Sixteen-year-old James Polk survives surgery to remove urinary stones.

1813 Polk begins his formal education at Zion Church Academy.

1814 Polk attends the Bradley Academy in Murfreesboro and finishes first in his class.

1816 Polk enters the University of North Carolina as a sophomore.

1818 Polk graduates with honors from the University of North Carolina.

1819 Polk studies law with Felix Grundy in Nashville.

1820 Polk passes the bar exam and opens a law practice in Columbia, Tennessee. Polk becomes the clerk of the Tennessee State Senate in Murfreesboro.

1823 Polk begins his service in the Tennessee state legislature.

1824 Polk marries Sarah Childress.

1825 Polk begins his first term in the U.S. House of Representatives.

1828 Polk helps Andrew Jackson win his campaign for the presidency.

1835 Polk is elected Speaker of the U.S. House of Representatives.

1839 Polk is elected governor of Tennessee.

1844 Polk is elected president of the United States.

1845 Andrew Jackson dies at the Hermitage. Texas is admitted to the Union as the twenty-eighth state.

1846 Polk negotiates the Oregon Treaty with Great Britain, achieves tariff reduction, and creates the independent treasury. Congress declares war on Mexico.

1848 Polk signs the Treaty of Guadalupe Hidalgo, ending the Mexican War.

1849 Polk returns to Nashville, Tennessee, after his presidential term ends. Polk dies of cholera on June 15 at the age of fifty-three.

1891 Sarah Polk dies in Nashville at the age of eighty-seven.

SOURCE NOTES

7 Eugene Irving McCormac, *James K. Polk: A Political Biography* (Berkeley: University of California Press, 1922), 2.

9 *James K. Polk Memorial*, 2004, http://www.ah.dcr.state.nc.us/sections/hs/polk/polk.htm. (March 2004).

12 Charles Sellers, *James K. Polk, Jacksonian* (Princeton, NJ: Princeton University Press, 1957), 13.

13 Ibid., 28.

16 Ibid., 43.

19 McCormac, 5.

23 Margaret Truman, *First Ladies* (New York: Random House, 1995), 97.

29 McCormac, 14.

43 Ibid., 9.

51 Robert Caro, *Master of the Senate* (New York: Alfred A. Knopf, 2002), 17.

51 Ibid.

51 Ibid., 19–20.

52 Ibid., 136.

53 Sellers, 365.

53 McCormac, 152.

55 Ibid., 246.

55 Sellers, 379.

58 Ibid., 447.

58 Ibid.

59 McCormac, 207.

64 Ibid., 232.

66 Ibid., 239.

67 Ibid., 248.

71 Ibid., 282.

72 Ibid., 319.

74 Ibid., 320.

74 Ibid., 319.

75 Ibid., 327.

75 Ibid., 324.

75 Milo Milton Quaife, ed., *The Diary of James K. Polk, Book II* (Chicago: Chicago Historical Society, 1910), 490.

77 Martha McBride Morrel, *Young Hickory: The Life and Times of James K. Polk* (New York: Dutton, 1949), 252.

80 McCormac, 329.

80 Ibid., 328.

85 Michael Beschloss, ed., *American Heritage Illustrated History of the Presidents* (New York: Crown, 2000), 147.

89 Thomas M. Leonard, *James K. Polk: A Clear and Unquestionable Destiny* (Wilmington, DE: SR Books, 2001), 77.

92 Richard C. Wade, Howard B. Wilder, and Louise C. Wade, *A History of the United States* (Boston: Houghton Mifflin Co., 1972), 287.

92 Carl Sandburg, *Abraham Lincoln: The Prairie Years* (New York: Harcourt, Brace, & Co., 1926), 367.

93 Quaife, 103–104.

93 Ibid., 104.

96 James M. McPherson, ed. *To the Best of My Ability: The American Presidents* (New York: Dorling Kindersley, 2000), 89.

96 Quaife, xxxi.

97 Charles A. McCoy, *Polk and the Presidency* (New York: Haskell House, 1973), 212.

103 Ibid., 218.

103 McPherson, 89.

BIBLIOGRAPHY

Baller, Paul F., Jr. *Presidential Candidates.* New York: Oxford University Press, 1981.

Bergeron, Paul H. *The Presidency of James K. Polk.* Lawrence: University Press of Kansas, 1987.

Beschloss, Michael, ed. *American Heritage Illustrated History of the Presidents.* New York: Crown, 2000.

Bumgarner, John Reed. *Sarah Childress Polk: A Biography of the Remarkable First Lady.* Jefferson, NC: McFarland & Co., 1997.

Caro, Robert. *Master of the Senate.* New York: Alfred A. Knopf, 2002.

Christman, Margaret C. S. *1846: Portrait of the Nation.* Washington, DC: Smithsonian Institution Press, 1996.

DeBruhl, Marshall. *A Life of Sam Houston.* New York: Random House, 1993.

DeGregorio, William A. *The Complete Book of U.S. Presidents.* New York: Barricade Books Inc., 1994.

Henry, Robert Selph. *The Story of the Mexican War.* New York: Random House, 1993.

Kunhardt, Phillip B., Jr., Phillip B. Kunhardt III, and Peter W. Kunhardt. *The American President.* New York: Riverhead Books, 1999.

Leonard, Thomas M. *James K. Polk: A Clear and Unquestionable Destiny.* Wilmington, DE: SR Books, 2001.

Mayo, Edith P., ed. *The Smithsonian Book of the First Ladies: Their Lives, Times, and Issues.* New York: Henry Holt, 1996.

McCormac, Eugene Irving. *James K. Polk: A Political Biography.* Berkeley: University of California Press, 1922.

McCoy, Charles A. *Polk and the Presidency.* New York: Haskell House, 1973.

McPherson, James M., ed. *To the Best of My Ability: The American Presidents.* New York: Dorling Kindersley, 2000.

Morrel, Martha McBride. *Young Hickory: The Life and Times of James K. Polk.* New York: Dutton, 1949.

Nelson, Anson, *Sarah Childress Polk: Wife of the Eleventh President of the United States.* 1892. Reprint, New York: American Political Biography Press, 1994.

Quaife, Milo Milton, ed. *The Diary of James K. Polk, Books I and II.* Chicago: Chicago Historical Society, 1910.

Sandburg, Carl. *Abraham Lincoln: The Prairie Years.* New York: Harcourt, Brace & Co., 1926.

Sellers, Charles. *James K. Polk, Continentalist.* Princeton, NJ: Princeton University Press, 1966.

———. *James K. Polk, Jacksonian.* Princeton, NJ: Princeton University Press, 1957.

Siegenthaler, John. *James K. Polk.* New York: Henry Holt and Co., 2004.

Truman, Margaret. *First Ladies.* New York: Random House, 1995.

Wade, Richard C., Howard B. Wilder, and Louise C. Wade. *A History of the United States.* Boston: Houghton Mifflin Co., 1972.

Weaver, Herbert, ed. *Correspondence of James K. Polk.* Nashville: Vanderbilt University Press, 1969.

Further Reading and Websites

Behrman, Carol. *Andrew Jackson*. Minneapolis: Lerner Publications Company, 2003.

Bennett, Barbara Peterson. *Sarah Childress Polk, First Lady of Tennessee and Washington*. New York: Nova Science Publishers, Inc., 2002.

Donovan, Sandy. *James Buchanan*. Minneapolis: Lerner Publications Company, 2005.

Feldman, Ruth Tenzer. *The Mexican-American War*. Minneapolis: Lerner Publications Company, 2004.

Gaines, Ann Graham. *James Polk: Our Eleventh President*. Chanhassen, MN: Child's World, 2002.

James K. Polk: 11th President of the United States.
http://www.jameskpolk.com.
Produced by the James K. Polk Ancestral Home, this website includes biographies of James and Sarah Polk, information on the home and its exhibits, and other educational materials.

James K. Polk Memorial.
http://www.ah.dcr.state.nc.us/sections/hs/polk/polk.htm.
Created by the Polk Memorial in North Carolina, this website includes a biography of James Polk, along with information on special events at the memorial.

Lillegard, Dee. *James K. Polk*. Chicago: Children's Press, 1988.

Mills, Bronwyn. *The Mexican War*. New York: Facts on File, 1992.

Roberts, Jeremy. *Zachary Taylor*. Minneapolis: Lerner Publications Company, 2005.

Sinnott, Susan. *Sarah Childress Polk*. Children's Press: New York, 1998.

Tibbitts, Alison Davis. *James K. Polk*. Berkeley Heights, NJ: Enslow Publishers, 1999.

Uschan, Michael. *Westward Expansion*. San Diego: Lucent Books, 2001.

INDEX

abolitionists, 45, 93
Adams, John Quincy, 37, 72;
    congressman, 45; 1828 election, 36;
    president, 27, 31, 32, 33, 34, 35
American Revolution, 11, 12, 38, 62,
    64, 69
Armstrong, Robert, 70

Bancroft, George, 65, 95
banks, pet, 41; Bank of the United
    States, 40, 78
Bell, John, 43–44, 45
Boone, Daniel, 62
Buchanan, James, 81, 84, 94

Calhoun, John C., 41, 42, 51
California, 78, 86–87, 95
Carroll, William, 25, 26, 27
Carson, Kit, 87
Childress, Anderson, 16
cholera, 98, 99
Civil War, 82, 102
Clark, William, 62–63
Clay, Henry: election of 1844, 67, 69,
    70; famous orator, 50, 51, 67; Polk's
    political enemy, 41, 58, 59, 61, 65;
    secretary of state, 32
committees (House), 43, 47; Foreign
    Affairs, 35; Ways and Means, 37
Crockett, Davy, 26, 27, 37

dark horse, 66
Democratic Party, 21, 38, 44, 49,
    56–57, 58, 59; Democratic National
    Convention (1844), 60, 61, 64–66;
    Democratic National Convention
    (1848), 97; split in, 71
depression, 48–49, 57
duels, 39, 48

election of 1844, 67–70
Electoral College, 31, 33, 36, 69

Free Soilers, 97
Frémont, John C., 87, 92

gag rules, 47, 48
gaslights, 79
Grundy, Felix, 20, 21, 27

Harris, Jeremiah George, 53
Harrison, William Henry, 57
Houston, Sam, 33, 90

Jackson, Andrew, 21–22, 31, 32, 34,
    38–39, 55, 65; death, 79; 1824
    election, 27; 1828 election, 35, 36;
    Hermitage, 59, 64, 71, 79; influence
    on Polk, 17, 23, 71; leader of
    Democratic Party, 49, 52, 53, 59,
    60; nickname, 38, 44, 67, 79;
    president, 36–37, 38, 40–41, 42, 44,
    48, 86, 103
Jefferson, Thomas, 17, 21, 62
Jones, "Slim" Jimmy, 58

Knox, John, 9

land speculation, 19
Lewis, Meriwether, 62–63
Lincoln, Abraham, 92, 103
Louisiana Purchase, 62

manifest destiny, 60, 61, 63, 83, 87
McDowell, Ephraim, 7, 8, 15; office, 6
Mecklenburg County, North Carolina,
    9, 11–12, 100
Mexican-American War, 89–95, 100, 103
Monroe Doctrine, 85

Nashville Union, 53, 59, 64
Native Americans, 11, 63
nullification, 48, 51

orators, famous, 50–51

ABOUT THE AUTHOR

Carol H. Behrman was born in Brooklyn, New York, graduated from City College of New York, and attended Columbia University's Teachers' College, where she majored in education. For many years, Behrman taught grades five through eight at the Glen Ridge Middle School in New Jersey. She has written more than twenty books, fiction and nonfiction, for children and young adults, as well as seven writing textbooks. Her other titles include *Fiddler to the World: The Inspiring Life of Itzhak Perlman*, *The Indian Wars*, *Roberto Clemente*, *Andrew Jackson*, *John Adams*, *Thomas Jefferson*, and *Miss Dr. Lucy*, the story of the first woman dentist in America. Behrman lives in Sarasota, Florida.
